ALISON ROCHE

Aerial view of Scarborough Castle, showing its commanding position on Castle Hill

CARBOROUGH CASTLE occupies one of the most dramatic of English Heritage sites. The massive grassy headland of Castle Hill stands some 300ft (92m) high, commanding spectacular views along the coast and inland towards the North York Moors.

The promontory is a natural fortress, surrounded by precipitous cliffs and connected to the mainland by only a narrow neck of land. Defensive settlements were built here during the late Bronze and early Iron Ages, well over 2500 years ago. Towards the end of their occupation of Britain the Romans used the headland as a lookout station, one of several along the Yorkshire coast, and a Saxon monastery later flourished for a while. In the tenth century the Vikings settled below the cliff and named the town after their leader.

Two centuries later the Plantagenet kings also recognised the strength of the site and built a castle, which was maintained for over 450 years as a royal power base in the north. Although besieged a number of times it was never taken by military might alone. The most serious damage was inflicted by Roundhead cannon during the English Civil War and by German naval guns in 1914.

The castle dominates the town and harbour below it. Over the centuries the royal borough of Scarborough has had a chequered history. In the time of Edward III great flocks of sheep were kept on the nearby moors, and the town became an important centre of the English wool trade. Mineral springs were discovered in the 1620s, as a result of which the town developed in the eighteenth and nineteenth centuries into a popular place for taking the waters and the new pastime of sea bathing. At that time up to 200 fishing boats would follow the herring shoals along the coast, and it is said that the area was the haunt of smugglers.

Nowadays Scarborough is a first-class holiday resort, one of the largest on the east coast. Nevertheless, the castle ramparts and Henry II's shattered keep are constant reminders of the town's sterner and more turbulent past.

TOUR OF THE CASTLE

TOUR ROUTE
From ticket office to
Roman signal station

*From the ticket office,
climb the paved
approach towards the
keep . . .*

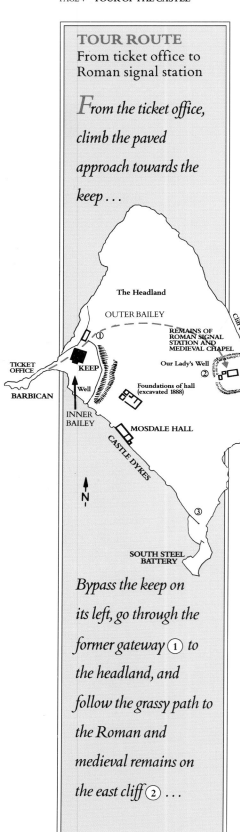

*Bypass the keep on
its left, go through the
former gateway ① to
the headland, and
follow the grassy path to
the Roman and
medieval remains on
the east cliff ② . . .*

THE HEADLAND

The headland covers about 16 acres (6.5ha), or eight football pitches. Like much of this area of Yorkshire, it consists of tough limestone grits around which the softer rocks have been eroded to form North and South Bays. It is surrounded by cliffs up to 300ft (92m) high, with access from the mainland by only a narrow neck of land. This has made it a natural defensive position since the earliest times.

In the medieval period the headland was used as a huge outer bailey (defended enclosure). The nature of the site makes Scarborough unusual in that, unlike most castles, the outer bailey was not the first line of defence. It was used largely as an enclosure where animals were kept and vegetables grown to help with the garrison's provisions. Here also the lords of the castle indulged in sport and pageantry; it is known that tilting was part of the festivities when Edward I held court at Scarborough in 1275.

Roman Signal Station

Around AD370 Britain, like many parts of the Roman Empire, was under attack by barbarian raiders. A local countermeasure was to build a signal station on Scarborough headland, one of five such outposts along the North Yorkshire coast. Its purpose was to watch out for hostile ships and send warning by smoke signals to the cavalry base at Malton and thence to the legionary headquarters at York.

The outline of the tower can be seen in the centre of the site Ⓐ, although it is partly obscured by later medieval buildings. It was about 42ft (12.8m) square and built of stone. There were two or three storeys, surmounted by an iron basket for the beacon fire.

The tower stood in a courtyard some 100ft (30.5m) square. This was defended by a *wall with a gate* Ⓑ on the landward side and a *wide deep ditch* Ⓒ. The eastern side of the compound has long since fallen into the sea because of cliff erosion.

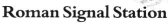

Roman Signal Station as it might have appeared in the fourth century, from a drawing by Alan Sorrell

Scarborough headland from South Bay. South Steel Battery can be seen half way down the cliff

Early Chapel

In about AD 1000 a *small chapel* (D) was built on the remains of the Roman signal station, utilising part of the ruined walls. It seems to have been associated with a Saxon monastery then situated on the headland, and was probably destroyed when Norsemen under Hardrada occupied the site in 1066.

The present barrel vault (arched roof) is part of the twelfth century rebuilding, although the doorway dates from the sixteenth century. The brick water tank inside was constructed by the Army in the eighteenth century.

Later Medieval Chapel

A *second chapel* (E) was built around 1140 when William le Gros erected the first castle. Fragments of carved stone found during excavations show that it was highly decorated. It seems to have lasted unaltered until the early fourteenth century, when the west end was shortened to make room for an attached *priest's house* (F). The house's *latrine* (G) and the sill of the connecting door to the nave are clearly visible.

The *carved stone grave slab* (H) in the nave dates from the fourteenth century.

Tudor Dwelling

After the Reformation further extensions were made to the medieval chapel and the

site was converted into a *house* (J), although little trace of this is now visible.

The Well of Our Lady

In the corner of the Roman compound is the *Well of Our Lady* (K). In medieval times it was thought to be miraculous because the water always stood within 10ft (3m) of ground level. It now seems to be dry for most of the year, although it occasionally contains water in winter.

The well was said to have healing properties, possibly because it contained the same beneficient minerals as the spa waters which later made the town famous.

The keep from the southeast, *showing the steps to the forebuilding*

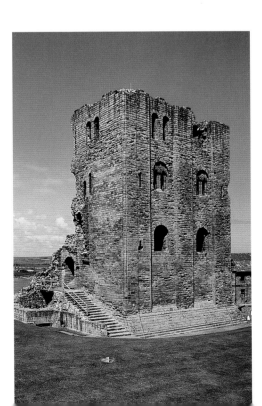

TOUR ROUTE
From ticket office to
Roman signal station

*Cross the grassy ditch
and enter the remains of
the Roman signal
station . . .*

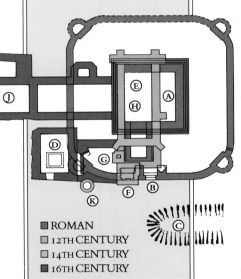

■ ROMAN
□ 12TH CENTURY
□ 14TH CENTURY
■ 16TH CENTURY

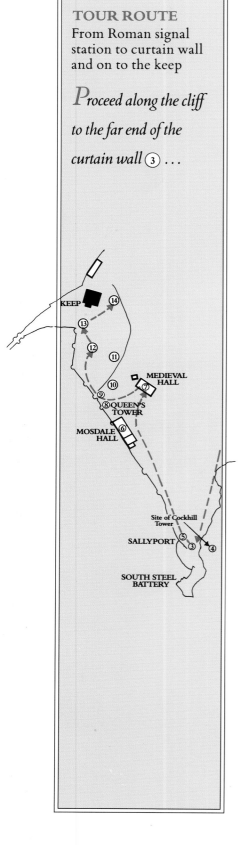

TOUR ROUTE
From Roman signal
station to curtain wall
and on to the keep

*Proceed along the cliff
to the far end of the
curtain wall ③ …*

The curtain wall from the keep

THE CURTAIN WALL

Beyond the end of the curtain wall once stood the *Cockhill Tower* ④. Tradition says it housed political prisoners, including the Quaker, George Fox, in 1665–66. By 1750 it had fallen into the sea which then washed the foot of the cliffs.

Down some steps near the end of the curtain wall is a *postern gate* or *sallyport* ⑤ through which the garrison could make surprise attacks on besiegers. The gate is probably medieval in origin, but was modified during the Civil War. Outside, flights of steps lead down to the remains of the South Steel Battery and from there to the harbour. The battery dates from about 1643, but was reconstructed for twelve guns in 1746. The steps and path are protected on their outer side by a wall with loopholes for shooting through; this probably dates from the fourteenth century, although it was greatly altered during the seventeenth and eighteenth centuries.

The curtain wall was the castle's main defence to the west and south, extending along the entire landward face of the cliff to foil any attack across *Castle Dykes*. It has been much repaired and strengthened over the centuries, with towers and buttresses being added at different dates. The parts built before 1300 are distinguished by

shallow pilaster buttresses (rectangular columns built against the wall to give it additional strength) at irregular intervals on the outside face.

The towers in this section of the curtain wall are hollow. They probably date from the time of Henry III and reflect the new theories of military architecture adopted during the thirteenth century. As the tower were hollow, archers could defend the base of the wall at ground level and the towers' half-round shape helped to deflect missiles from outside. They also provided extra accommodation when necessary.

The remains of a considerable *residential complex* ⑥ mark the site of *Mosdale Hall*. This was built originally by King John, who always preferred comfortable surroundings. It was rebuilt at the end of the fourteenth century by John Mosdale, governor of the castle from 1397. After the Jacobite Rebellion of 1745 the hall was again reconstructed, this time in red brick, as a barrack for 120 officers and men. The barrack stood until December 1914 when it was shelled by German battle cruisers. Its demolition exposed the foundations of the original medieval undercroft, which was used for storage. Above it would have been the hall itself with a chamber for the lord at the southeast end.

To the right are the foundations of a large *medieval hall* ⑦ which were exposed by the Army during the 1880s and re-excavated in 1973. The hall was probably built in the late twelfth century, the beginning of the period when the lords were moving out of their draughty keeps into more comfortable accommodation in the bailey. It was a substantial building for its period, although it may have been modified and enlarged later. At the end nearest the keep was a separate complex of service rooms which included a kitchen.

The *ruined tower* ⑧ is known as the *Queen's Tower,* supposedly after the wife of Richard III. Note the latrine in the wall on the left.

Pass into the castle's *inner bailey* by the steps ⑨. To the right on either side of the ditch are the remains of an early *stone bridge* ⑩, including the foundations of a *gate tower* on the inner side.

German bombardment of 1914, with shells exploding on the castle walls

Foundations of the medieval hall in the outer bailey, excavated in 1888

Mosdale Hall from the outer bailey. The hall was rebuilt several times before being destroyed in 1914

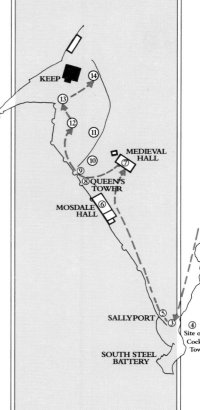

TOUR ROUTE
From Roman signal station to curtain wall and on to the keep

Continue along the curtain wall towards the keep …

KEEP

⑭ ⑬ ⑫ ⑪ ⑩ ⑨ ⑦ MEDIEVAL HALL ⑧ QUEEN'S TOWER ⑥ MOSDALE HALL

SALLYPORT ⑤ ③ ④ Site of Cockhill Tower

SOUTH STEEL BATTERY

Pass into the castle's inner bailey by the steps ⑨ …

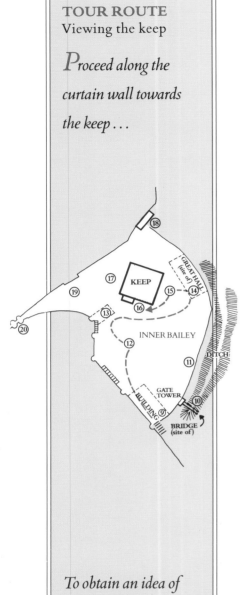

TOUR ROUTE
Viewing the keep

Proceed along the curtain wall towards the keep . . .

To obtain an idea of what the keep once looked like, view it first from the east (15), the only reasonably complete side . . .

THE INNER BAILEY

The inner ward or bailey of the castle stretches some 112yd (103m) north to south and 73yd (67m) east to west.

Henry II constructed his new castle between 1158 and 1168. On the landward side of the headland a curtain wall prevented an attack across the natural ravine of Castle Dykes. The keep was further protected by cutting off the western angle of the headland with a curved ditch and bank. This was at first topped by a palisade (fence of strong upright tibers) and later, probably towards the end of the twelfth century, by a *stone wall* (11).

The inner bailey would once have been filled with domestic offices and some workshops, although the more noisy and offensive of these would have been situated in the outer bailey. The foundations of some of these buildings can be seen along the inside of the curtain wall.

*Section of the **curtain wall** bordering the inner bailey, showing the iron basket for the beacon fire*

The towers along this section of the curtain wall are solid, and are therefore early. Probably they date from the time of King John (1199–1216). Note the iron basket for a beacon fire on top of the wall. The earliest reference to a beacon being kept ready at the castle occurs in 1523.

The *castle well* (12) dates from the time of Henry II. It is a remarkable piece of medieval engineering, although it no longer contains water. The well head is 7ft (2.1m) in diameter and the shaft is over 150ft (46m) deep. The stone lining descends 68ft (20.7m) before giving way to natural rock.

At the corner of the *curtain wall* (13) are the foundations of more early medieval buildings. The rounded section on the left was a bread oven, the stones of which have been discoloured pink by the heat. The rest of this complex included the castle's kitchen, which was usually situated away from the keep for fear of fire.

The joist holes for the upper floor of a *large building* (14) can be seen in the face of the inner bailey wall. This was probably a great hall, built towards the end of the twelfth century as a more comfortable alternative to the hall in the keep.

THE KEEP

The style of Henry II's great tower was strongly influenced by the massive Norman keeps built earlier in the century.

Nearly 100 years after the Battle of Hastings, the Normans had subdued the country and made England their home. Some consideration could therefore be given to comfort as well as defence, and this factor was beginning to appear at Scarborough. Before long, castles such as Orford (built c1170) incorporated kitchens, private accommodation and other domestic amenities as a matter of course.

The keep was badly damaged during the English Civil War when Parliamentary cannon brought down the entire western wall. The interior is not accessible to the public.

Much of the façade has been refaced in modern times and some of the windows ave been restored, but enough remains to how that the keep was once a fine example of its period.

Externally it is about 55ft (17m) square. t originally stood 100ft (30.5m) high with a urret at each corner, although it now verages only 85ft (26m).

In the centre of each wall is a broad buttress which rose the full four storeys. The corners are also strengthened by buttresses, the angles ornamented with three-quarter round mouldings.

The west side of the keep was destroyed in 1645. Traces of latrine chutes can be seen just above the plinth

SPEARHEAD PHOTOGRAPHY

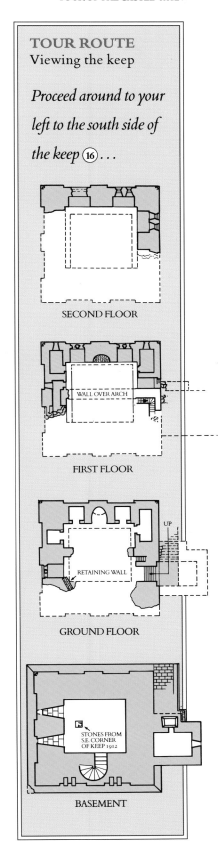

TOUR ROUTE
Viewing the keep

Proceed around to your left to the south side of the keep ⑯ . . .

SECOND FLOOR

WALL OVER ARCH

FIRST FLOOR

UP

RETAINING WALL

GROUND FLOOR

STONES FROM S.E. CORNER OF KEEP 1912

BASEMENT

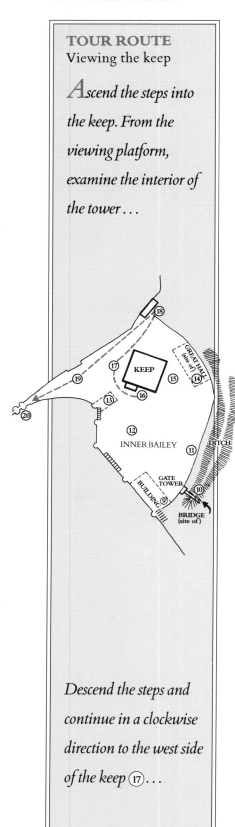

TOUR ROUTE
Viewing the keep

Ascend the steps into the keep. From the viewing platform, examine the interior of the tower . . .

Descend the steps and continue in a clockwise direction to the west side of the keep (17) *. . .*

The arrangement and design of the window apertures reflect the function of each floor. At the top they are simple pairs of round-headed windows, but on the important second floor they are more elaborate with double lights and twin shafts contained in half-round arches. The windows of the first floor would have been similar, their size showing there was little fear of an attack reaching the keep itself. At various places slits can be seen which served both for illumination and as arrow loops.

Note the massive sloping plinth on which the keep stands. This provided a solid foundation, made it more difficult to undermine the wall, and would also deflect rocks dropped from the battlements into the legs of anyone attacking the base of the tower.

Forebuilding

Like most twelfth-century keeps, that at Scarborough had no doors at ground level. The entrance was on the first floor and was protected by a strong forebuilding (16). This made it more difficult for attackers to break in and also provided an imposing entrance (an important factor when a lord's castle reflected his status).

Although the forebuilding is now completely ruined, its general dimensions can be seen from the foundations and the traces of projecting masonry on the south wall. Its base was 30ft by 20ft (9.2m by 6.1m) and it stood some 40ft (12.2m) high.

The forebuilding was the keep's first line of defence. Attackers ascending the broad flight of stone steps would be subjected to missiles dropped on them from the battlements. In the wall above the top of the steps are indications that there was a gallery over the entrance door.

The basement of the forebuilding was on two levels (note the joist holes in the wall on the left). It may have been a prison, though the remains of a window splay in the south wall make this unlikely. More probably it was just a rather gloomy lodging. The aperture and sloping slab under the steps was a latrine.

Above the basement was the keep's entrance chamber, an ornate room designed to impress visitors. Above that was

Detail of the east wall of the keep, *including a fine window on the second floor*

probably the castle chapel, which was usually situated on the forebuilding's top floor. The entrance to this can be seen above the door to the keep.

Basement

This was a plain chamber used only for storage.

It had no exterior doors, the only access being from the floor above by a broad spiral staircase which rose to the full height of the building. The lowest steps of this can be seen in the middle of the wall on the left. Its position is unusual, as the stairs of most keeps were situated in corner turrets.

In the far wall are the splays for two small windows, although one of these does not penetrate to the outside.

Note the great thickness of the walls, about 15ft (4.6m) on the ruined side and 11 to 12ft (3.5m) elsewhere.

First Floor

The first floor of the keep, *the level of the viewing platform,* would have been the original great hall. This is where the castle's resident constable received visitors, held local courts and conducted estate business.

It was a single large room about 32ft (9.8m) square, spanned by a flying arch, the broken ends of which can be seen in the far wall and above to the right. The arch supported a wall which divided the second floor into two chambers. This was a significant architectural development, as earlier keeps were usually divided from top to bottom by a solid central wall.

By day the great hall was very busy, full of officials and servants going about their everyday affairs. Before more comfortable accommodation was built in the inner and outer baileys, it was also the place where many of the castle's occupants ate and slept, for only the most important people had the luxury of a private room, however small. Meals were taken at trestle tables which could be stowed away when not in use, with everyone seated on benches in strict order of rank. At night most people simply curled up on the floor, wrapped in their cloaks.

Second Floor

This was divided into two chambers by a wall supported on the arch below.

The ornate windows show that it was an important floor, a suite reserved for the governor or for the king on one of his progresses around the country. Try to imagine it with the walls plastered and painted, and hung with tapestries to keep out the draughts.

Note the large round-backed fireplaces in the wall on the right on both first and second floors, an improvement on the braziers of earlier times. The herringbone pattern of the brickwork was thought to be more resistant to heat.

Both floors had a number of small private chambers within the thickness of the walls, and latrines which discharged through chutes to the foot of the tower.

From the west side of the keep ⑰ the interior can again be viewed through the shattered wall. Just above the plinth on either side of the central staircase are traces of the latrine chutes which discharged onto the ground.

The house at the north end of the inner bailey wall was the *Master Gunner's House* ⑱. It was built in 1748 as part of the Army's reoccupation of the headland. From the time of Henry II the castle defences grew outwards towards the narrow neck of land which separates Castle Hill from the mainland, although the present walls on either side date from the thirteenth century. They funnel down to a narrow, easily defended entrance which could be covered by firepower from the keep above.

A *modern bridge* ⑳ now crosses the natural ravine of Castle Dykes. This has replaced the two drawbridges which once guarded the crossing, the outer one of which survived into the nineteenth century. The outer drawbridge was raised from the two towers between the spans of the present bridge; the other was raised from the inner side of the ditch.

The keep seen from above North Bay

SPEARHEAD PHOTOGRAPHY

TOUR ROUTE
Viewing the keep

Leave the keep and return to the paved approach . . .

Descend the path ⑲ towards the barbican . . .

TOUR ROUTE
From the keep to
the barbican

*Cross the bridge to the
outer defences of the
barbican . . .*

*As you approach the
entrance, you will end
the tour at the last part
of the castle to be built,
the barbican or fortified
outer gateway . . .*

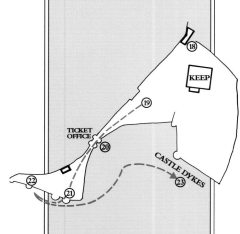

*Pass through the gate
and view the defences
from the outside.*

THE BARBICAN

The barbican was completed around 1350, although it has been much repaired and rebuilt over the centuries. It was situated on the landward side of the ravine to stop attackers getting close enough to the keep to mount a full-scale assault, and to prevent them using primitive artillery. However, by the time of the Civil War more powerful cannon could pound the castle from a distance and the barbican was the scene of fierce fighting.

There seems always to have been some kind of outwork here, though not on the scale to be seen now. It is first mentioned in 1174–75, and the foundations of an early rectangular tower have been found on the site. During the thirteenth and fourteenth centuries much attention was paid to making castle entrances impregnable, so much so that the gatehouse replaced the keep in most castles that were built after that time.

In 1243 Henry III ordered "a new tower before the Castle Gate" as part of his review of the defences. A hundred years later this was reconstructed more or less in its present form by Edward III.

The barbican consists of a gateway protected by two massive *half-round towers* ㉑. The approach is covered by a *flanking wall* ㉒ strengthened by two smaller towers, all of which would originally have been topped by battlements. The towers' curved outer faces were stronger than the old square towers, the corners of which could often be brought down by mining.

Consider the difficulties facing anyone attacking the gateway. First they would have to struggle up the hill beneath the flanking wall, under fire from the walkway behind the wall and the two wall towers.

The gate itself was recessed so that it could be defended from the main towers on either side, and would have been reinforced by a portcullis. Above are machicolations (apertures through which stones and other missiles could be dropped).

As you leave the castle, look back and consider it from an attacker's point of view. The main impression is of how the defences impress themselves on the skyline high above the approaches.

It is worth exploring the *cliff path* ㉓ along Castle Dykes to the South Steel Battery and from there to the harbour. From there you can appreciate the futility of mounting an assault anywhere except at the narrow entrance, and that is covered by the barbican and double drawbridge. Dominating everything is Henry II's ancient keep.

From any angle the castle's strength is obvious, and it is scarcely surprising that it remained impregnable to military attack throughout its long history.

The steep approach to the barbican is protected by a gateway and two massive half-round towers

THE HISTORY

EARLY SETTLEMENTS

Scarborough headland was inhabited long before the Normans built the present castle. Neolithic remains and Bronze Age barrows can be found all over North Yorkshire, although excavations on the headland itself suggest that the earliest habitation began in the late Bronze Age or early Iron Age.

During this period primitive peoples were migrating from Europe to the east coast of England. Some time between 900 and 700BC settlements were established on the extreme east of the headland and near the site of the medieval hall in the outer bailey. No traces of these are now visible,

although some fifty small rubbish pits were excavated in the 1920s. These revealed a variety of artifacts which indicate that their owners came from the lower Rhine area of Germany.

Much later the Romans established a small signal station on the exposed eastern cliff. Towards the end of the fourth century AD the edges of the Roman Empire were crumbling beneath the attacks of barbarian raiders. The headland site was one of five outposts set up between the Tees and Flamborough Head around AD370 to watch out for Pictish and Saxon ships.

After the Roman withdrawal the headland appears to have been unoccupied until a Saxon monastery was established

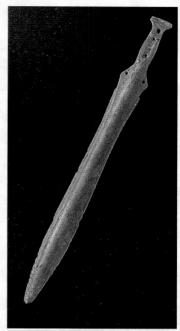

Bronze Age sword found during excavations on the headland in 1984

The castle as it might have been around 1350, from a painting by Ivan Lapper. The gaps shown in the curtain wall may not have existed

*The marriage of **Edward III** (1327—77)|to Isabella, daughter of Philip IV of Spain*

BRITISH MUSEUM

Henry II from a tomb effigy at Fontevrault, France

there in the seventh or eighth century. An early Christian chapel was built on the ruins of the Roman watchtower around the year 1000.

By this time a small fishing settlement had grown up around the harbour. During the ninth century England was subjected to constant Viking attacks, and in the north particularly many of these erstwhile raiders settled permanently and eventually became Christians. In AD966 one such burh (settlement) was set up in the shelter of the headland by the Viking leaders Kormak and Thorgils. Thorgils was nicknamed Skarthi, or Harelip, and the town he helped establish became known as *Skarthi's burh* or Scarborough.

In 1066 the throne of England was claimed by the three greatest warriors of the age. The outcome of the battle between King Harold and William of Normandy is well known, but just before Hastings the main threat was from Harald Hardrada, the ferocious King of Norway. After ravaging the east coast, Hardrada landed at Scarborough before sailing on to defeat and death at Stamford Bridge. A Norse saga tells how he sacked and burned the town by building a huge bonfire on the headland and rolling bundles of blazing hay down on to the houses below. Almost certainly the chapel on the east cliffs was destroyed at the same time.

THE FIRST FORTIFICATION

The first reference to a castle at Scarborough occurs during the disastrous reign of King Stephen (1135–54). The local lord was William le Gros, Earl of Aumâle. In 1138 he played a prominent part in the defeat of the Scots at the Battle of the Standard, near Northallerton. Soon|afterwards he was created Earl of Yorkshire and became an important power in the land.

Although le Gros had other greater castles, he recognised that Scarborough headland was an immensely strong position commanding a fine harbour. He strengthened the western cliffs with a palisade or wall, and built a gate tower to command the approaches. No trace of this now remains, although it probably stood near the present keep.

Le Gros held Scarborough throughout Stephen's reign, a period known as *the Anarchy* because it consisted largely of intermittent civil war and struggles for the throne.

THE PRESENT CASTLE

When Henry II came to the throne in 1154 his first priority was to reduce the power of the barons. One of those who resisted was William le Gros, but within a few months he was forced to surrender and the castle was taken away from him.

Henry kept Scarborough for himself, probably to maintain a royal power base in Yorkshire. The site was already a natural fortress, but he set about making his new acquisition the most powerful castle in the area. His work can be dated precisely, for expenses totalling some £650 appear in the Pipe Rolls from 1158–68.

Scarborough was the earliest castle for which Henry II was entirely responsible. Le Gros's gate tower was pulled down and a strong stone keep erected in its place. The curtain wall on the cliff edge was rebuilt and strengthened, and an early barbican probably defended the narrow approaches. A ditch and bank were cut across the angle of the headland to form an inner bailey.

The outer defences were repeatedly strengthened and improved over the centuries. The cliffs made it impossible for attackers to get close except at the easily defended entrance, and the castle was never taken except by trickery or starvation (see pages 16, 19 and 23).

The keep as it might have been around 1175, from a painting by Ivan Lapper ▷

THE CASTLE IN MEDIEVAL TIMES

Throughout the medieval period the Plantagenet kings attached much importance to maintaining their most powerful stronghold in Yorkshire, although the exposed nature of the site often made it an expensive liability.

King John stayed at Scarborough on four occasions between 1201 and 1216, spending over £2000 (an enormous sum for those days) on the curtain wall, the garrison and general maintainance. He probably built the original Mosdale Hall against the wall of the outer bailey as a more comfortable residential complex.

Cannons such as this formed a vital part of the castle's defences

MICHAEL HOLFORD

Edward II, *from an alabaster tomb effigy in Gloucester Cathedral*

BRITISH LIBRARY

Edward III *(1327–77) as founder of the Order of the Garter. From the Stowe Manuscript*

In 1278 it was estimated that £2200 would be needed for urgent repairs to several roofs, the wooden bridge between the barbican and the main gate, and 1100yd (1000m) of curtain wall.

In 1312 Scarborough Castle was besieged for the first time. The castle's governor was Piers Gaveston, a favourite of King Edward II. The upstart Gaveston had infuriated the barons by his arrogance, and a confederation was formed to put an end to his influence. Gaveston defended the castle against many assaults but was forced to surrender when his provisions ran out. He was promised a safe conduct to London for trial, but on the way he was seized by his implacable enemy the Earl of Warwick and summarily beheaded.

The next few years saw a renewal of the Scottish invasions which had plagued northern England since the twelfth century. The raids increased after the English defeat at Bannockburn (1314) and for a while Northumberland, Durham and even

Henry III also spent large amounts of money on the defences. In 1243–45 he gave orders for completing the great gateway of the barbican, and probably also built most of the hollow towers which strengthen the outer bailey's curtain wall. Nevertheless, by the time Edward I held court at the castle in 1275 the defences had already deteriorated.

Detail of the **curtain wall**

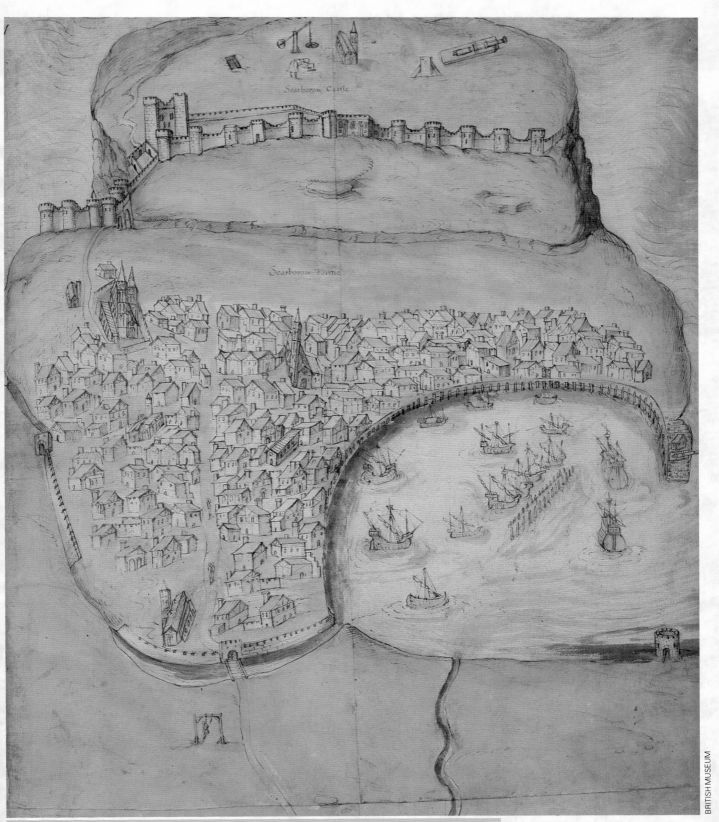

Scarborow Castle

Scarborow Towne

Plan of Scarborough *town and castle drawn in the time of Henry VIII*

*Engraving of Scarborough's **South Bay and the Castle** by Samuel and Nathaniel Buck*

Yorkshire were under threat. In 1318 a particularly penetrating raid reached Scarborough itself.

Edward III's ambitions lay more towards France than Scotland, and Scarborough was attacked several times during the Hundred Years War because of its importance to the English wool trade. The great barbican was reconstructed around 1343, leaving the outline of the castle much as it is today.

Despite these efforts to maintain the outermost defences, the castle continued to decline steadily into decay. In 1393 it was stated that repairs would cost at least £2000.

In 1484 Richard III visited the castle on his progress around the country. One of the towers in the curtain wall is called the Queen's Tower, supposedly after his wife Anne, although it was apparently

known by this name well before that date.

During the reign of Henry VIII Scarborough was attacked several times by France and Scotland, although the most serious threat came from a rebellion in the

*Part of a **fifteenth-century medieval cross shaft** from the chapel on the headland*

Scarborough was an important centre of the English wool trade and scenes such as this would have been a familiar part of the local landscape. From a sixteenth-century manuscript

north in 1536. Protesters against Henry's religious changes and the suppression of the monasteries were organised into an army by Robert Aske. However, reports that this Pilgrimage of Grace besieged the castle for twenty days seem to have been invented by the constable, Sir Ralph Eure, who was himself accused the following year of plundering the castle by stripping lead from the roofs and cheating the garrison of its wages.

Scarborough Castle changed hands twice in 1557, both times without serious bloodshed. Sir Thomas Stafford tried to use Mary Tudor's unpopular marriage with Philip II of Spain to rally support against her. He and thirty companions strolled into the town one market day, disguised as peasants but with arms concealed beneath their rags. They overwhelmed the sentries at the gate and seized the castle. Stafford proclaimed himself Protector of the Realm but the support he expected did not materialise. He surrendered within a week and was taken to London for execution on Tower Hill.

Some work was carried out on the castle in 1581–84, but within thirty years it was again in so ruinous a state that the cost of repairs was estimated at over £4000. Continuing a policy of offloading unwanted and expensive castles, King James I sold Scarborough to the Earl of Holderness in 1624. The castle was restored to the Crown in 1662.

*A **Bellarmine** jug (sixteenth or seventeenth century) found on Castle Hill*

*Old print of the **North Gate** of Scarborough Castle*

DONALD INNES

Sir Matthew Boynton, *MP for Scarborough, who took over as Governor of the castle after its surrender in 1645*

CIVIL WAR SIEGES,
1645 and 1648

The most severe sieges that the castle underwent in its long history were during the English Civil War, when it defied Parliament on two occasions. Although the decisive battles of the war were fought in open country, many of England's ancient castles were recommissioned and often resisted attacks for months at a time. Once again Scarborough's strength was demonstrated in the way it held out against weapons unimaginable to its medieval builders.

The First Siege
February to July 1645

Few people expected that the differences between King Charles I and his Parliament would result in a full-scale war. Nevertheless, by 1642 the deadlock was such that both sides made preparations to protect their positions.

Parliament commissioned Sir Hugh Cholmley, a local landowner, to hold Scarborough and the surrounding area, but in March 1643 he went over to the King.

In July 1644 Parliamentary forces defeated the King at nearby Marston Moor and moved to within a few miles of

Fighting for the barbican *in the siege of 1645, from an illustration by Victor Ambrus*

Scarborough. Cholmley prevaricated long enough to provision the town and castle, and it was not until January 1645 that he came under direct attack from Sir John Meldrum and an army of 3000 Scots.

The town itself fell in February, the loss of the harbour denying the garrison any chance of retreat or resupply by sea. Nevertheless, for a further five months the Royalists defended themselves resolutely against Parliamentary assaults. Meldrum set up batteries of cannon to pound the barbican and Henry II's 500 year old keep. The largest gun in the country, the *Cannon Royal,* was installed inside St Mary's Church at the foot of the hill, hurling its 60 lb balls at the ancient defences through the east window of the chancel.

Thwarted at the front, the besiegers tried to attack the castle from the seaward side of the headland. Part way up the cliffs,

*Painting by Dirck Stoop showing the procession of **Charles II** from the Tower of London to Westminster in 1661*

Meldrum himself met with an accident. His hat blew off, and while trying to recover it *"his coat was blown over his head, and, striving to get it down, the wind blew him over head foremost down the cliff amongst the rocks and stones at least steeple height."* Not surprisingly, after the fall Meldrum *"lay speechless for three days,"* but was apparently up and about again within six weeks.

The constant bombardment eventually split the ancient keep in two. The west wall collapsed, the stones and rubble tumbling down to block the path to the barbican. Another determined assault here was repelled in fierce hand-to-hand fighting as the defenders hurled the fallen stones down on their enemies with deadly effect. By now the gatehouse was so battered that the garrison had to withdraw, returning only to beat off further attacks. Meldrum himself was fatally wounded leading an attack on the southeast corner of the headland, and for ten days the gatehouse lay unheld by either side.

Silver tokens *such as these were used as money during the siege of Scarborough in the Civil War*

The siege was renewed under Sir Matthew Boynton, MP for Scarborough. By July the garrison's position was desperate. Some 180 of the 200 men under Cholmley's command were sick or wounded, most of them unable to move, and all were starving.

Recognising that further resistance was pointless, Cholmley negotiated an honourable surrender. The garrison's survivors left the castle on 25 July 1645, although the gatehouse was so damaged that it was impassable and a hole had to be cut in the wall to let the defenders out. Parliament voted a day of thanksgiving and £5000 to repair the damage.

The Second Siege,
September to December 1648

The Civil War flared up again in 1648. By this time Sir Matthew Boynton had died, to be succeeded as governor of the castle by his son.

Like Cholmley before him, Colonel Boynton found Parliament a difficult master. Most of the Army's pay was well in arrears, and in July 1648 he and his discontented garrison declared for the King.

Once again Parliament found itself having to retake a fortress it had thought was its own. The town and harbour fell on 15 September and Scarborough Castle's second great siege of the Civil War began in earnest.

The garrison held out for three months behind the newly repaired defences, but eventually exhaustion and starvation took their toll. Faced with the onset of winter Boynton surrendered the castle to Colonel Bethell on 15 December.

Less forgiving this time, the Council of State for the Commonwealth ordered the castle's demolition the following year. It seems, however, that the damage was already so great that it was unnecessary for the order to be carried out.

J M W Turner's watercolour of South Bay
BRITISH MUSEUM

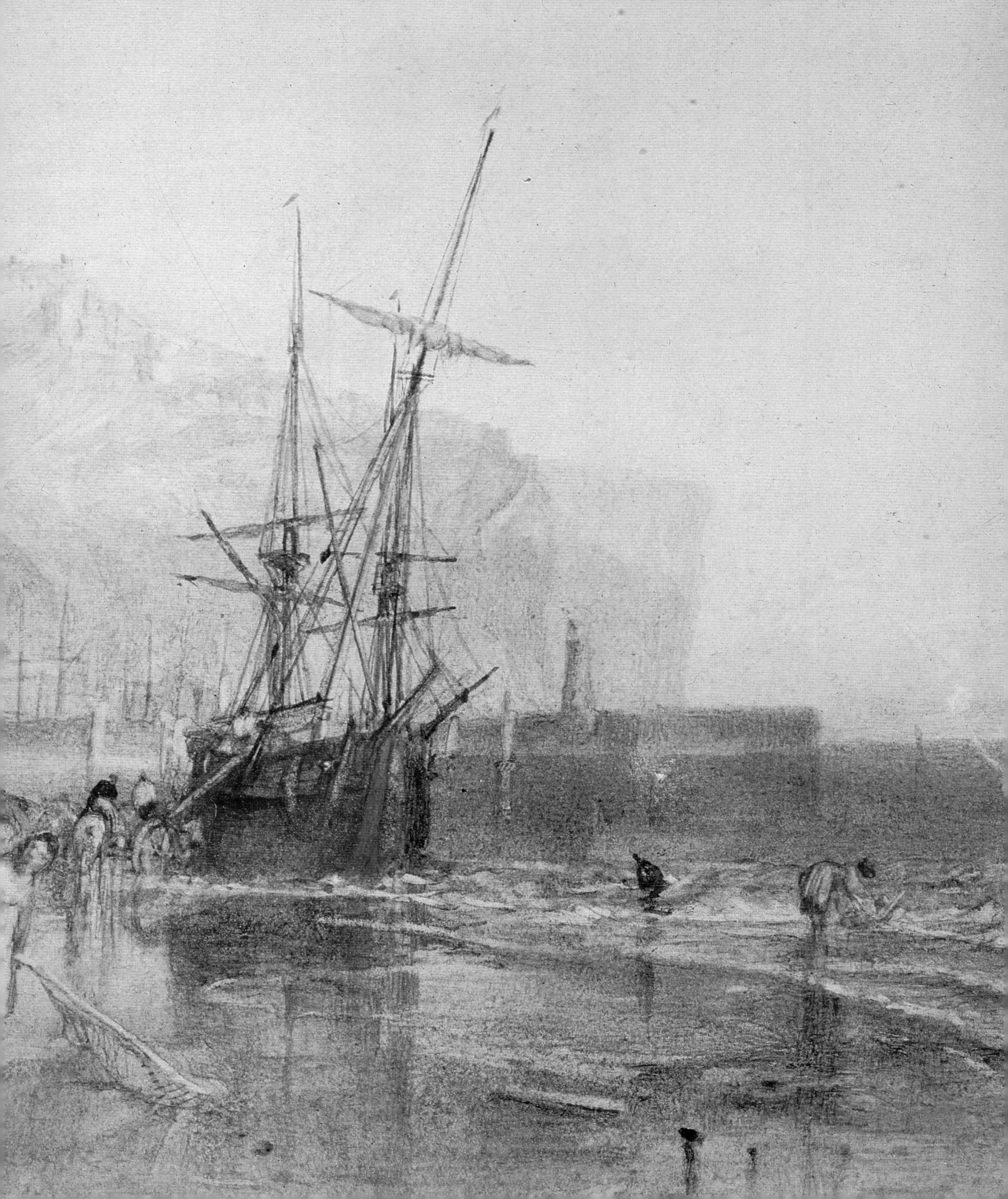

Richard III (1483–85) visited the castle during his short reign

PRISON . . .

After the Civil War, the castle's outer buildings were used as a barrack. During the 1650s an artillery position was maintained in the South Steel Battery.

At this time the castle also became a prison for those who offended the government. It had of course housed other prisoners throughout its history. Edward I's Welsh hostages were held there in 1295, as were Scottish prisoners from Stirling in 1311.

Probably the castle's best known prisoner in later times was George Fox, the founder of The Society of Friends (the Quakers). He was held in the Cockhill Tower from April 1665 until September

...66, the longest of his eight terms of ...nprisonment. Although Fox had paid out ...oney for better conditions, as was usual in ...ose days, he was moved to a worse room ...here *"I had neither chimney nor firehearth. ...his being to the seaside and much open, the ...ind drove the rain in forcibly, so that the water ...me up over my bed and ran about the room ...at I was fain to skim it up with a platter."*

... AND BARRACK

...1746, following the alarm caused by the ...cobite Rebellion the previous year, a ...arrack for 120 officers and men was built ...n the ruins of Mosdale Hall. The castle ...ecame a powder magazine for the district and the South Steel Battery was refurbished.

A permanent garrison was again established at the castle following the threat of invasion during the Napoleonic Wars, and French prisoners were kept there from 1796 onwards. Detachments of the Army were stationed on the headland until the late nineteenth century.

The barrack lasted until 16 December 1914 when the town and its ancient castle were shelled by the German battle cruisers *Derfflinger* and *Von der Tann*. Its subsequent demolition exposed the medieval foundations of Mosdale Hall.

In 1920 responsibility for the castle passed to the Office of Works and its successors. Since 1984 it has been in the care of English Heritage.

Seal of Scarborough from a seventeenth-century silver badge

*A nineteenth century engraving of **Scarborough Castle***

THE SOCIETY OF FRIENDS

George Fox, *the founder of the Quakers, was imprisoned at Scarborough in 1665. His fortitude impressed even his jailers. "He is as stiff as a tree, and as pure as a bell," said one, "for we could never move him." From a painting at Swarthmore College, Pennsylvania*

HRONOLOGY

c900—700BC	Late Bronze Age and early Iron Age settlements on the headland
cAD370	Roman signal station built near the east cliff
AD966	Settlement established by Thorgils (Skarthi)
cAD1000	Earliest chapel on headland
1066	Town sacked by Norsemen under Hardrada
	Battle of Hastings, accession of William the Conqueror
1135	Death of Henry I, accession of Stephen
c1135—38	First fortifications on Castle Hill, gate tower and curtain wall built by William le Gros
1154	Death of Stephen, accession of Henry II
1159—68	Present keep built by Henry II
1201—16	Defensive work by John
c1240—50	Extensive work to defences and barbican by Henry III
1275	Edward I holds court at the castle
1312	Siege of Piers Gaveston
1318	Town and castle threatened by the Scots
1343—45	Barbican and outer defences completed by Edward III
1377	Mercer (Scottish pirate) attacks the harbour but is routed by Alderman Philpot of London
1424—29	Extensive repairs by Henry VI
1484	Richard III visits the castle
1536	Castle allegedly besieged by the Pilgrimage of Grace
1557	Castle seized by Thomas Stafford, but is recaptured for the Crown within a week
1624	Castle sold by James I
c1626	Discovery of mineral springs by Mrs Farrer
1645	First siege of the Civil War; castle surrendered on honourable terms
1648	Second siege of the Civil War
1662	Castle returned to the Crown
1665—66	Imprisonment of George Fox
1746	Construction of barrack
1890	Large fall of cliff
1914	Castle and town shelled by German warships
1920	Site taken over for the nation by the Office of Works
1984	Castle placed in the care of English Heritage